ALBERT EINSTEIN

LEGENDS AND LEGACIES

THE BIOGRAPHY OF
ALBERT EINSTEIN

Published by
Rupa Publications India Pvt. Ltd 2023
161-B/4, Gulmohar House,
Yusuf Sarai Community Centre,
New Delhi 110049

Sales centres:
Bengaluru Chennai
Hyderabad Kolkata Mumbai

Copyright © Rupa Publications India Pvt. Ltd 2024

The views and opinions expressed in this book are the author's own and the facts are as reported by him which have been verified to the extent possible, and the publishers are not in any way liable for the same.

All rights reserved.
No part of this publication may be reproduced, transmitted, or stored in a retrieval system, in any form or by any means, electronic, mechanical, photocopying, recording or otherwise, without the prior permission of the publisher.

P-ISBN: 978-93-6156-845-9
E-ISBN: 978-93-6156-712-4

Second impression 2026

10 9 8 7 6 5 4 3 2

Printed in India

This book is sold subject to the condition that it shall not, by way of trade or otherwise, be lent, resold, hired out, or otherwise circulated, without the publisher's prior consent, in any form of binding or cover other than that in which it is published.

Contents

Introduction	7
Early Life (1879-1896)	9
Formative Years and Education (1896-1905)	13
The Miracle Year (1905)	18
Academic Career and Rise to Fame (1905-1919)	23
Life in Berlin and the Weimar Republic (1914-1933)	27
Years in America (1933-1945)	32
Later Years and Legacy (1945-1955)	37
Personal Life and Character	44
Impact on Science and Society	51
Einstein's Impact on Education and Outreach	57
Einstein's Views on Politics and Social Issues	61
Einstein's Influence on Modern Cosmology and Astrophysics	65
Einstein's Nobel Prize and Recognition	72
Einstein's Unfinished Work and Unanswered Questions	76
Conclusion	79

Introduction

Albert Einstein is widely regarded as one of the most influential and iconic figures in the history of science. His revolutionary ideas transformed our understanding of the universe, and his name has become synonymous with genius and intellectual prowess. Born in the late 19th century and living through some of the most tumultuous periods of the 20th century, Einstein's contributions extended far beyond the realm of physics. He became a symbol of curiosity, creativity, and the relentless pursuit of knowledge.

Einstein's significance in science is unparalleled. He introduced concepts that challenged the traditional Newtonian framework and reshaped modern physics. His theories of relativity, both special and general, altered the way we think about space, time, and gravity. These ideas not only advanced scientific thought but also paved the way for numerous technological advancements, from nuclear energy to GPS systems.

In addition to his scientific work, Einstein's unique personality and public presence made him a cultural icon. His distinctive appearance, characterized by his wild hair and thoughtful demeanor, has been immortalized in countless photographs and caricatures. He was not just a brilliant scientist but also a humanitarian who spoke out on issues of war, peace, and social justice. His voice carried weight on matters far beyond the laboratory, influencing political leaders and the general public alike.

Einstein's life was a fascinating journey marked by significant milestones. From his early years in Germany and Switzerland, where he displayed an extraordinary aptitude for mathematics and physics, to his later years in the United States, where he continued to contribute to scientific thought and engage in public advocacy, Einstein's story is one of remarkable achievements and enduring impact.

Einstein's journey was not just about scientific discovery; it was also about the pursuit of knowledge and the application of that knowledge for the betterment of humanity. Through his work and his actions, Einstein exemplified the power of intellectual curiosity and the importance of using one's talents for the greater good. This introduction sets the stage for a deeper exploration of a man whose life and work continue to inspire and influence people around the world.

1

Early Life (1879-1896)

Birth and Family Background

Albert Einstein was born on March 14, 1879, in the city of Ulm, in the Kingdom of Württemberg, which was part of the German Empire. His parents, Hermann Einstein and Pauline Koch, were of Jewish descent but were not particularly religious. Hermann was an engineer and salesman who initially ran a featherbed business before shifting to the electrical industry. Pauline managed the household and was known for her musical talent, particularly her piano playing. The Einstein family valued education and intellectual pursuits, creating an environment conducive to young Albert's early intellectual curiosity.

> **Fun Fact**
> Albert Einstein was born with an abnormally large head, and his grandmother initially thought he was deformed. Fortunately, he grew into it!

Childhood in Germany and Switzerland

When Albert was one year old, his family moved to Munich, where Hermann and his brother Jakob founded Elektrotechnische Fabrik J. Einstein & Cie, a company that manufactured electrical equipment based on direct current. Despite early success, the business eventually faced financial difficulties, leading the family to move several times during Albert's childhood.

Albert had a quiet and introspective nature and was slow to speak, which concerned his parents. In fact, he didn't start speaking fluently until he was around four years old. This led to a family nickname, "der Depperte," meaning "the dopey one." Despite this slow start, he displayed a deep curiosity about the natural world. His early years in Munich were marked by a solitary disposition and a love for constructing mechanical devices and models.

Max Talmud

At age ten, Albert was introduced to science and philosophy by Max Talmud (later Max Talmey), a young medical student who dined weekly with the Einsteins. Talmud lent Albert books that greatly influenced his thinking, including works by Kant and Euclid. Albert's passion for science and mathematics was further ignited.

> **Fun Fact**
> Albert was known to have a temper tantrum at school when he was frustrated with the rigid and authoritarian methods of teaching!

When Albert was 15, his family moved to Italy after their business failed. Albert stayed behind in Munich to finish his education but soon followed them to Italy, feeling isolated and unhappy at school.

Early Education and Fascination with Science and Mathematics

Albert's formal education began at the Luitpold Gymnasium in Munich, where he found the rigid teaching methods stifling. His teachers often regarded him as lazy and unfocused, failing to see his potential. Despite this, Albert excelled in mathematics and showed an early fascination with complex scientific concepts. He taught himself algebra and Euclidean geometry over a single summer and began studying calculus at the age of twelve.

A turning point in Albert's early education came when he discovered a book on geometry, which he called his "sacred little geometry book." This discovery sparked a lifelong passion for mathematics and theoretical physics. Despite struggling with the rote learning and authoritarian discipline of his school in Munich, he nurtured his curiosity through self-study and personal experiments.

In 1894, at the age of 15, Albert decided to leave Germany and join his family in Italy. He continued his education in Switzerland, where he found a more encouraging and liberal academic environment.

Fun Fact

Albert loved playing the violin and often said that music helped him think. He named his violin "Lina."

He completed his secondary education at the Cantonal School in Aarau, where his teachers recognized and supported his intellectual abilities. It was during this period that Albert wrote his first scientific paper, discussing the nature of the ether and the implications of its existence on physical theories.

The Influence of His Family and Mentors

Albert's family played a crucial role in nurturing his intellectual development. His mother, Pauline, was a talented pianist and instilled in him a love for music, especially the violin, which remained a lifelong passion. His father, Hermann, though not scientifically inclined, encouraged Albert's interest in science and provided him with the tools to explore his curiosity. One notable gift was a compass, which fascinated Albert with its mysterious behavior and sparked his interest in magnetism.

Max Talmud, the medical student who dined with the Einstein family, became an important mentor. He introduced Albert to key scientific and philosophical texts, broadening his horizons and deepening his understanding of complex concepts. Talmud's guidance was instrumental in shaping Albert's early intellectual pursuits.

> **Fun Fact**
>
> While in Aarau, Albert stayed with the Winteler family and fell in love with Jost Winteler's daughter, Marie. Although their romance didn't last, it was a significant part of his adolescence.

Another significant influence was Jost Winteler, a teacher at the Cantonal School in Aarau. Winteler recognized Albert's potential and provided a supportive and stimulating environment. The Winteler family also became close friends with the Einsteins, further fostering Albert's development.

These early years were formative for Albert Einstein, laying the foundation for his future achievements. His family's support, the mentors who guided him, and his innate curiosity and determination all contributed to the making of a genius who would go on to change the world.

2

Formative Years and Education (1896-1905)

Attending the Swiss Federal Polytechnic in Zurich

In 1896, at the age of 17, Albert Einstein enrolled in the Swiss Federal Polytechnic School in Zurich, known today as ETH Zurich. Initially, he attended a special high school program in Aarau, Switzerland, to qualify for entry, since he had dropped out of his German high school without a diploma. This decision was pivotal, as it exposed him to a liberal and stimulating academic environment that contrasted sharply with the rigid educational system he had experienced in Germany.

At the polytechnic, Einstein met several lifelong friends and colleagues, including Marcel Grossmann, who later played a crucial role in Einstein's development of the general theory of relativity. The atmosphere at the polytechnic was intellectually vibrant, encouraging free thought and innovative ideas, which suited Einstein perfectly.

Fun Fact

Einstein's entrance exam results for the polytechnic showed an excellent performance in mathematics and physics, but he performed poorly in French, chemistry, and biology. This prompted the polytechnic to admit him on the condition that he completed his secondary education first.

Development of His Early Scientific Ideas

During his time at the polytechnic, Einstein's fascination with physics deepened. He immersed himself in the works of physicists such as James Clerk Maxwell, whose electromagnetic theory particularly intrigued him. The polytechnic's emphasis on independent study allowed Einstein to explore these ideas freely, often spending hours in the library poring over scientific texts and engaging in discussions with his peers.

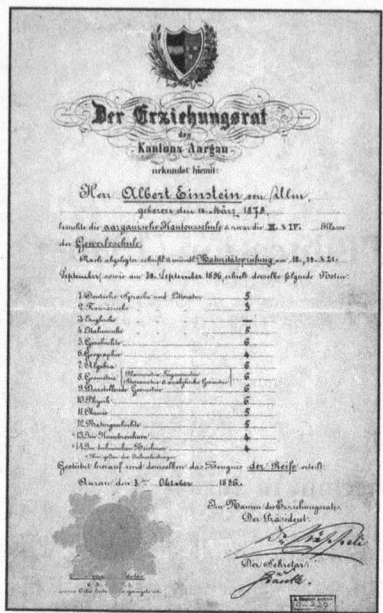

Albert Einstein's secondary school grades

Einstein began to develop some of his early scientific ideas that would later revolutionize physics. He explored concepts like electromagnetism and thermodynamics, questioning and testing the accepted theories of the time. His innovative thinking and refusal to accept conventional wisdom laid the groundwork for his future groundbreaking work.

In addition to the formal curriculum, Einstein's curiosity led him to conduct experiments and develop theoretical insights outside the classroom. He would later reflect on this period as crucial for his intellectual growth, as it allowed him to cultivate the habit of independent inquiry and critical thinking.

Fun fact: Einstein often skipped classes that he found uninteresting or poorly taught, preferring to study on his own or with a small group of like-minded friends. He relied heavily on Marcel Grossmann, who shared notes and helped Einstein prepare for exams.

Struggles and Achievements During His University Years

Einstein's university years were not without challenges. He struggled with the rigid structure of the educational system and had a rocky relationship with some of his professors, who did not appreciate his nonconformist attitude and frequent absences from class. One of his professors, Heinrich Weber, even advised him to drop out, believing that Einstein lacked the discipline to succeed in academia.

Despite these struggles, Einstein excelled in subjects that truly interested him. He developed a reputation among his peers for his sharp intellect and deep understanding of complex scientific concepts. However, his nonconformist approach and poor attendance led to mediocre grades in subjects he found unengaging.

After graduating in 1900 with a diploma in mathematics and physics, Einstein faced a difficult job market. His reputation for being headstrong and independent did not endear him to potential employers. For two years, he struggled to find stable employment, working as a private tutor and even considering changing careers. This period of uncertainty was marked by financial difficulties and personal frustration.

> **Fun Fact**
> Einstein applied for several academic positions without success. He even contemplated taking a job as an insurance clerk at one point, highlighting the challenging start to his career despite his evident potential.

Relationship with Mileva Marić

During his time at the polytechnic, Einstein met Mileva Marić, a Serbian physicist and one of the few women studying at the institution. Their relationship began as a deep intellectual friendship, built on a shared passion for science and extensive discussions about physics. Mileva was highly intelligent and ambitious, and their relationship quickly evolved from friendship to romance.

Mileva played a significant role in Einstein's early academic life, providing both intellectual and emotional support. They often studied together, discussing scientific theories and working through complex problems. There is considerable debate among historians about the extent of her contribution to Einstein's work, with some suggesting that she collaborated with him on his early papers, including those published in his annus mirabilis of 1905.

Einstein with Mileva Marić

Their relationship faced several challenges, including disapproval from Einstein's family, who were wary of Mileva's Serbian Orthodox background and the fact that she was older than Albert. Despite these challenges, the couple remained close and eventually married in 1903. They had two sons, Hans Albert and Eduard.

Their marriage, while initially happy, eventually became strained due to personal and professional pressures. Mileva's own scientific ambitions were largely sidelined as she took on the role of wife and mother, while Einstein's career began to ascend rapidly. Nonetheless, during their early years together, Mileva provided crucial support that helped Einstein navigate his formative academic challenges.

These formative years at the Swiss Federal Polytechnic were crucial in shaping Einstein's future. Despite facing numerous challenges, his relentless curiosity and innovative thinking set the stage for the remarkable achievements that would soon follow, including his famous papers of 1905. His relationship with Mileva Marić added a personal dimension to this critical period, highlighting the interplay between his personal and professional life.

> **Fun Fact**
>
> Einstein and Mileva had an illegitimate daughter, Lieserl, born in 1902. Very little is known about her fate, and it remains one of the enigmas of Einstein's personal life. Some believe she was given up for adoption, while others think she may have died young.

3

The Miracle Year (1905)

Einstein's Annus Mirabilis (Miracle Year)

The year 1905 marks a pivotal moment in the history of science, famously referred to as Albert Einstein's "annus mirabilis" or miracle year. Working as a third-class patent examiner at the Swiss Patent Office in Bern, Einstein devoted his evenings and weekends to scientific pursuits, using his spare time to ponder some of the deepest mysteries of physics. Despite lacking the academic resources and collaborations typical of university settings, Einstein's keen intellect and relentless curiosity propelled him to produce four revolutionary papers that fundamentally reshaped the foundations of physics.

The Four Groundbreaking Papers

> **Fun Fact**
> Einstein's explanation of the photoelectric effect was initially met with skepticism by many physicists, including Max Planck, the father of quantum theory. It took several years for the scientific community to fully embrace his revolutionary idea.

1. The Photoelectric Effect

Einstein's first paper, published in March 1905, "On a Heuristic Viewpoint Concerning the Production and Transformation of Light," revolutionized the understanding of light. In this work, he proposed that light could be understood as consisting of discrete packets of energy, or quanta, which he termed photons. This idea challenged the prevailing wave theory of light proposed by Maxwell and others. By explaining the photoelectric effect—where light shining on a material ejects electrons—Einstein provided compelling evidence for the quantum nature of light. This work laid the foundation for quantum mechanics and earned him the Nobel Prize in Physics in 1921.

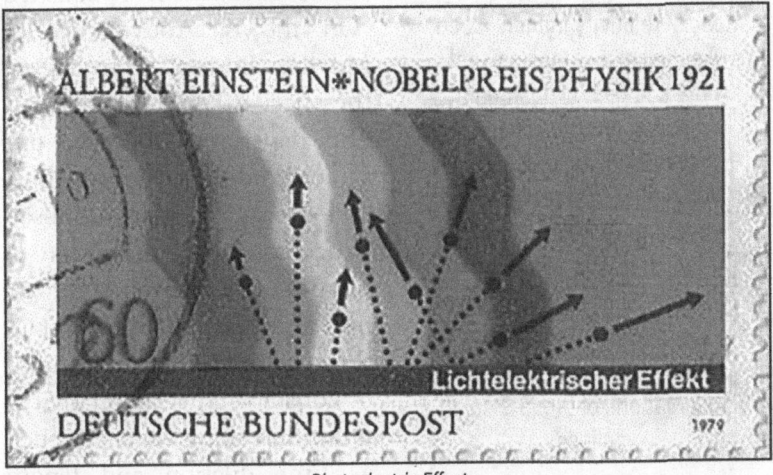

Photoelectric Effect

2. Brownian Motion

Published in May 1905, Einstein's second paper, "On the Movement of Small Particles Suspended in a Stationary Liquid as Required by the Molecular-Kinetic Theory of Heat," provided a theoretical explanation for Brownian motion. This phenomenon, where small particles suspended in a fluid exhibit random motion, had puzzled scientists for decades. Einstein applied statistical mechanics to show that Brownian motion

Fun Fact

French physicist Jean Perrin's experimental confirmation of Einstein's theoretical predictions on Brownian motion in 1908 solidified Einstein's reputation as a leading physicist and convinced skeptics of the reality of atoms.

was caused by the collision of visible particles with the invisible molecules of the surrounding liquid. His theoretical insights confirmed the existence of atoms and molecules, which had been debated since ancient times, and provided empirical evidence supporting atomic theory.

3. Special Relativity

In June 1905, Einstein published "On the Electrodynamics of Moving Bodies," introducing the special theory of relativity. This paper revolutionized our understanding of space, time, and energy. Einstein proposed two postulates: the laws of physics are the same for all non-accelerating observers and the speed of light in a vacuum is constant. Special relativity's groundbreaking concepts, such as time dilation and length

> **Fun Fact**
> Special relativity initially faced skepticism and took several years to gain widespread acceptance, despite its profound implications for physics. It required experimental confirmation, which was provided by subsequent experiments such as the Michelson-Morley experiment and the observations of the 1919 solar eclipse.

Special Relativity Formulae before 1940

contraction, challenged classical mechanics and provided a new framework for understanding the universe.

4. Mass-Energy Equivalence

Einstein's final paper of 1905, published in September, "Does the Inertia of a Body Depend Upon Its Energy Content?" introduced the concept of mass-energy equivalence. In this paper, Einstein derived the famous equation $E=mc^2$, which states that mass and energy are interchangeable and are related by the speed of light squared. This revolutionary concept fundamentally altered our understanding of energy and matter, providing the theoretical basis for nuclear physics and the development of atomic energy.

> **Fun Fact**
>
> The practical implications of $E=mc^2$ were not immediately apparent, but its significance became evident with the discovery of nuclear fission and the realization that even small amounts of mass could release enormous amounts of energy, as demonstrated in atomic bombs and nuclear reactors.

Reception and Initial Impact of His Work

The reception of Einstein's 1905 papers varied widely among physicists and the scientific community. While some immediately recognized the genius and novelty of his ideas, others were skeptical of the radical departures from established theories. Max Planck and other prominent physicists gradually came to support Einstein's work, recognizing its profound implications for physics and its potential to explain previously unexplained phenomena.

Soviet Postage depicting Einstein and his formula for mass-energy equivalence

Max Planck

Fun Fact

Einstein himself modestly referred to his 1905 papers as his "inventions," reflecting his playful and creative approach to scientific inquiry and problem-solving.

Einstein's papers from 1905 sparked a revolution in physics, fundamentally altering our understanding of the universe and laying the groundwork for modern physics. His concepts, such as the quantum nature of light, the existence of atoms and molecules, the relativity of space and time, and the equivalence of mass and energy, have had far-reaching implications across scientific disciplines, from quantum mechanics to cosmology.

The miracle year of 1905 marked the beginning of Albert Einstein's ascent to scientific fame and established him as one of the greatest minds in history. His groundbreaking contributions continue to inspire scientific research and technological innovations to this day, exemplifying the power of human curiosity and intellect in advancing our understanding of the natural world.

4

Academic Career and Rise to Fame (1905-1919)

Einstein's Career Progression Through Academia

In 1905, Albert Einstein was a relatively unknown employee at the Swiss Patent Office in Bern. Despite the mundane nature of his job, it allowed him ample time to engage in his true passion: theoretical physics. This year, often celebrated as Einstein's "Annus Mirabilis" or "Miracle Year," saw the publication of four groundbreaking papers in the prestigious scientific journal "Annalen der Physik." Each of these papers would fundamentally alter the landscape of physics.

The first paper addressed the photoelectric effect, explaining how light can eject electrons from a material. This work challenged the classical wave theory of light and introduced the revolutionary concept of light quanta, or photons. This discovery was so significant that it later earned Einstein the Nobel Prize in Physics in 1921.

His second paper dealt with Brownian motion, providing empirical evidence for the existence of atoms by explaining the erratic movement of particles suspended in a fluid. The third paper introduced the special theory of relativity, which redefined the concepts of space and time. Finally, his fourth paper presented the famous equation E=mc2E=mc^2E=mc2, which established the equivalence of mass and energy.

> **Fun Fact**
>
> When Einstein first applied for a teaching position, he was turned down. The University of Bern rejected his application for a lecturer position in 1907 because he had not yet completed a proper dissertation.

These papers cemented Einstein's reputation as a formidable intellect. In 1908, his growing recognition led to a position as a lecturer at the University of Bern. This was quickly followed by an appointment as an associate professor at the University of Zurich in 1909. Einstein's academic journey gained momentum, and in 1911, he was appointed full professor at the German University in Prague. A year later, in 1912, he returned to Zurich to teach at the prestigious ETH (Swiss Federal Institute of Technology). By 1914, Einstein had moved to Berlin to join the Prussian Academy of Sciences and took up a position at the University of Berlin. His academic rise was rapid, marked by his exceptional contributions to theoretical physics.

His office at University of Berlin

Development of the General Theory of Relativity

Einstein's special theory of relativity dealt with objects moving at constant speeds and fundamentally changed our understanding of space and time. However, Einstein was not content with just that; he sought to include gravity in his new framework. His quest to understand gravity led him to develop the general theory of relativity, a pursuit that occupied him from 1907 to 1915.

Einstein proposed a groundbreaking idea: gravity is not a force between masses but a curvature of space and time caused by mass and energy. This idea was revolutionary and required a new and complex mathematical framework to describe. Einstein's equations, encapsulated in the form $R_{\mu\nu} - \frac{1}{2} R g_{\mu\nu} + \Lambda g_{\mu\nu} = \frac{8\pi G}{c^4} T_{\mu\nu}$, described how matter and energy influence the curvature of spacetime.

After years of intense work, Einstein presented his general theory of relativity to the Prussian Academy of Sciences in Berlin in November 1915. His theory predicted phenomena that could be tested experimentally, such as the bending of light by gravity and the precession of the orbit of Mercury.

> **Fun Fact**
>
> Einstein initially struggled with the complex mathematics needed for his general theory of relativity. He received crucial assistance from his friend and mathematician Marcel Grossmann.

World War I and Its Impact on His Work

The outbreak of World War I in 1914 came shortly after Einstein's move to Berlin. The war had a profound impact on Europe, causing widespread devastation and significantly affecting Einstein's personal and professional life. Unlike many of his colleagues, Einstein was a pacifist and openly opposed the war. He was one of the few intellectuals who refused to sign the "Manifesto of the Ninety-Three," a document in which German scientists and scholars justified Germany's military actions.

Einstein's stance against the war made him a controversial figure, but he remained committed to his pacifist beliefs. Despite the challenging wartime conditions, which included food shortages and general unrest, Einstein continued his scientific work. His correspondence with scientists around the world helped maintain the exchange of ideas and collaboration during these tumultuous times.

Experimental Confirmation of General Relativity in 1919 and International Acclaim

> **Fun Fact**
> During World War I, Einstein helped found the German Democratic Party, which promoted peace and democracy. He also supported various humanitarian causes, including providing assistance to war victims.

Einstein's general theory of relativity made several bold predictions, one of the most famous being the bending of light by gravity. This could be observed during a solar eclipse, where the Sun's light would be blocked, allowing astronomers to measure the positions of stars near the Sun and compare them to their normal positions.

In 1919, British astronomer Sir Arthur Eddington led an expedition to observe a solar eclipse off the coast of West Africa. The results were groundbreaking: the observed positions of the stars confirmed Einstein's predictions. This experimental confirmation was a pivotal moment in the history of physics and marked a significant validation of Einstein's work.

News of the confirmation spread quickly and made headlines around the world. Einstein became an overnight sensation, and his theory of general relativity was hailed as a monumental scientific achievement. This newfound fame brought him international acclaim and established him as one of the greatest scientific minds of all time.

The period from 1905 to 1919 was transformative for Albert Einstein. His rise from a relatively unknown patent clerk to a world-renowned physicist was marked by his groundbreaking theories and their experimental confirmations. His work during these years revolutionized our understanding of the universe and solidified his legacy as one of the most influential scientists in history.

5

Life in Berlin and the Weimar Republic (1914-1933)

Move to Berlin and Work at the Prussian Academy of Sciences

In 1914, Albert Einstein made a significant career move by accepting an invitation to join the Prussian Academy of Sciences in Berlin. This was a prestigious position that not only provided him with an esteemed platform but also freed him from teaching obligations, allowing him to focus exclusively on his research. Berlin was a vibrant center for scientific research, attracting some of the brightest minds of the time. Einstein's appointment included a professorship at the University of Berlin, further cementing his status in the academic world.

Berlin offered Einstein unparalleled opportunities to collaborate with other leading scientists. His time there was marked by intense intellectual activity and significant breakthroughs. It was in Berlin that he completed the general theory of relativity in 1915, a monumental achievement that redefined our understanding of gravity, space, and time. The environment in Berlin, with its rich scientific community and resources, played a crucial role in fostering his groundbreaking work.

Einstein's contributions extended beyond his own research. He actively participated in the academic community, influencing the direction of scientific inquiry through his interactions and

> **Fun Fact**
> The special professorship Einstein received in Berlin was unique in that it allowed him to focus on research without the burden of teaching regular classes, a rare privilege at the time.

collaborations. His presence in Berlin helped establish the city as a hub of modern physics.

Personal Life, Including Marriage to Elsa Einstein

Einstein's personal life saw significant changes during his years in Berlin. In 1919, he divorced his first wife, Mileva Marić, with whom he had two sons, Hans Albert and Eduard. The divorce followed a period of separation, reflecting the personal and professional strains that had grown between them.

Albert and Elsa Einstein

Later that same year, Einstein married Elsa Löwenthal, his cousin. Elsa provided much-needed stability and support in his increasingly busy life. She managed his household, handled much of his correspondence, and accompanied him on many of his travels. Their relationship, while not without its challenges, offered Einstein a sense of personal security that he deeply appreciated.

Elsa's daughters from her previous marriage, Ilse and Margot, also became an important part of Einstein's life. He developed a close relationship with his stepdaughters, further enriching his family life. Despite the geographic distance and his demanding schedule, Einstein maintained a keen interest in the welfare of his sons, ensuring they received a good education and support.

Einstein's personal life was complex and often intertwined with his professional world. His relationships, both familial and romantic, influenced his work and provided a counterbalance to his intense intellectual pursuits.

> **Fun Fact**
> Elsa's dedication to Einstein was such that she even acted as a gatekeeper, managing the constant stream of visitors and admirers who sought to meet the famous scientist.

Engagement in Scientific, Political, and Social Issues

Einstein's time in Berlin was marked not only by scientific achievements but also by his active engagement in political and social issues. As a staunch pacifist, he was deeply opposed to Germany's militaristic policies and the horrors of World War I. He was one of the few intellectuals who publicly spoke out against the war, signing a manifesto advocating for peace. This stance made him a controversial figure in a society increasingly dominated by nationalist sentiment.

Hebrew University of Jerusalem

> **Fun Fact**
>
> Einstein's home in Germany was raided by the Gestapo, and his personal papers and possessions were confiscated. Despite these threats, he continued to speak out against the injustices perpetrated by the Nazi regime.

Einstein was also a committed Zionist, advocating for the cultural and intellectual revival of the Jewish people. He supported the establishment of a Jewish homeland in Palestine and played a significant role in fundraising for the Hebrew University of Jerusalem. His involvement in these causes was not just a matter of public speeches; he traveled extensively to garner support and used his influence to further these important social and political objectives.

His outspoken views on pacifism and Zionism, coupled with his Jewish heritage, made him a target for criticism and hostility, especially as anti-Semitic sentiments grew in Germany. Nonetheless, Einstein remained undeterred, leveraging his fame to promote peace, international cooperation, and social justice.

Einstein's engagement extended to various humanitarian causes. He supported efforts to help war victims and was involved in initiatives aimed at promoting global disarmament and fostering better international relations. His contributions to these causes reflected his deep commitment to making a positive impact on the world beyond the realm of theoretical physics.

Rise of the Nazi Party and Einstein's Emigration from Germany

The late 1920s and early 1930s brought dramatic changes to Germany with the rise of the Nazi party. As Adolf Hitler and his followers gained power, anti-Semitic rhetoric and violence escalated. Einstein, a prominent Jewish intellectual and outspoken critic of the Nazis, found himself in an increasingly precarious position.

The political climate became hostile, and Einstein was directly targeted by the Nazis. They denounced his theories as "Jewish physics" and launched a campaign to discredit him. In response to these threats and the dangerous environment, Einstein began to distance himself from Germany.

In 1933, when Hitler was appointed Chancellor of Germany, Einstein was abroad. Recognizing the severity of the situation, he decided not to return. He resigned from the Prussian Academy of Sciences and publicly condemned the Nazi regime. This was a courageous and decisive step that marked his final break with Germany.

Einstein initially sought refuge in Belgium, staying there for several months. He then moved to the United Kingdom before finally accepting an invitation to join the Institute for Advanced Study in Princeton, New Jersey. This move to the United States marked the beginning of a new chapter in his life, allowing him to continue his scientific work and advocacy from a safer environment.

Portrait at Princeton

The emigration was a significant turning point, not just for Einstein personally, but also for the broader scientific community. His departure from Germany symbolized the loss of intellectual talent that the Nazi regime's policies precipitated.

From 1914 to 1933, Einstein's life in Berlin was marked by profound scientific achievements, and active engagement in political and social issues. The rise of the Nazi party forced him to leave Germany, but his legacy continued to grow as he adapted to life in a new country, continuing his work and advocacy on a global stage. This period was one of intellectual activity and personal resilience, underscoring Einstein's unwavering commitment to his principles and his enduring impact on the world.

6

Years in America (1933-1945)

Move to the United States and Position at the Institute for Advanced Study in Princeton

In 1933, as the political situation in Germany deteriorated with the rise of the Nazi party, Albert Einstein made the life-altering decision to leave Europe. His first stops were in Belgium and the United Kingdom, where he sought temporary refuge. However, the invitation from the Institute for Advanced Study in Princeton, New Jersey, provided a stable and welcoming environment for his continued work. This institution, dedicated to theoretical research, was an ideal setting for Einstein, allowing him to focus on his scientific endeavors without the distractions of teaching obligations.

Einstein arrived in the United States in October 1933. His relocation was more than just a move; it represented a significant transition in his life and career. Princeton became his new home, where he found a community of like-minded scholars and a supportive environment for his research. The Institute for Advanced Study, under the leadership of Abraham Flexner, offered Einstein a position that allowed him the freedom to explore his theories without the constraints of traditional academic responsibilities.

Einstein's arrival in America was met with great enthusiasm. He was already a global celebrity, and his decision to settle in Princeton was seen as a significant gain for American science.

The town of Princeton itself welcomed Einstein warmly, and he quickly became a familiar figure in the community, known for his walks around town and his approachable nature.

> **Fun Fact**
> Upon his arrival in the United States, Einstein's celebrity status was such that he was often mobbed by reporters and admirers. He had to escape to Princeton via a different route to avoid the throngs of people waiting to greet him.

Jawaharlal Nehru with Albert Einstein at Princeton

Contributions to Quantum Mechanics and Unified Field Theory

During his time in Princeton, Einstein continued to contribute to various fields of physics, although his relationship with quantum mechanics was complex. He had made significant early contributions to the development of quantum theory, including his explanation of the photoelectric effect, which earned him the Nobel Prize in Physics in 1921. However, he remained deeply skeptical of the Copenhagen interpretation of quantum mechanics, famously summarized by his assertion that "God does not play dice with the universe."

Einstein's discomfort with the inherent randomness of quantum mechanics led him to explore alternatives. He engaged in numerous debates with prominent physicists such as Niels Bohr, who championed the Copenhagen interpretation. These debates were not merely academic; they highlighted fundamental philosophical differences about the nature of reality and the role of the observer in the physical world.

Einstein devoted a considerable part of his later career to developing a unified field theory, an ambitious attempt to reconcile the forces of nature within a single theoretical framework. He sought to unify general relativity, which describes the force of gravity, with electromagnetism. This quest was driven by his belief in a deterministic universe, where all physical phenomena could be explained by a comprehensive set of laws.

> **Fun Fact**
> Einstein often pondered his complex theories during long walks around Princeton. He would discuss his ideas with colleagues, students, and even interested townspeople, turning everyday conversations into deep explorations of scientific thought.

Despite his intense efforts and the occasional tantalizing hint of progress, Einstein was unable to achieve a fully satisfactory unified field theory. His work in this area, however, laid important groundwork and inspired future generations of physicists to continue exploring the unification of fundamental forces.

Role in the Development of Atomic Energy and the Manhattan Project

Einstein's years in America coincided with a period of rapid advancements in nuclear physics. Although Einstein himself was not directly involved in the technical development of nuclear weapons, his famous equation, $E=mc2E=mc^2E=mc2$, laid the theoretical foundation for the conversion of mass into energy, a principle crucial to the development of atomic bombs.

In 1939, concerned about the potential for Nazi Germany to develop nuclear weapons, Einstein signed a letter to President Franklin D. Roosevelt, drafted by physicist Leo Szilard. This letter urged the United States to accelerate its own atomic research, leading to the establishment of the Manhattan Project. The Manhattan Project was a top-secret U.S. government research initiative aimed at developing the first nuclear weapons. Although

Einstein did not work on the project himself, his letter is often credited with spurring the U.S. government to prioritize nuclear research.

Einstein later expressed regret about his indirect role in the development of nuclear weapons, advocating for the responsible use of atomic energy and emphasizing the need for international cooperation to prevent nuclear proliferation. He became an active voice in the movement for nuclear disarmament, recognizing the devastating potential of the weapons he had inadvertently helped bring into existence.

Leo Szilard

Advocacy for Civil Rights and World Peace

Einstein's commitment to social justice and peace remained steadfast throughout his years in America. He was an outspoken advocate for civil rights, lending his voice to the fight against racial segregation and discrimination. He formed a close friendship with African American civil rights leader W.E.B. Du Bois and supported the National Association for the Advancement of Colored People (NAACP).

Einstein used his celebrity status to bring attention to the injustices faced by African Americans. He publicly denounced

> **Fun Fact**
> Despite his pivotal role in alerting the U.S. government to the potential of nuclear weapons, Einstein was not granted the necessary security clearance to work on the Manhattan Project, largely due to his pacifist views and left-leaning political beliefs.

segregation and was a vocal supporter of efforts to end racial discrimination in the United States. His home in Princeton was known for welcoming African American guests at a time when such actions were not widely accepted. He frequently spoke out against the injustices faced by African Americans and used his platform to advocate for equal rights.

In addition to his advocacy for civil rights, Einstein was a passionate advocate for world peace. He spoke out against militarism and nationalism, and after the horrors of World War II, he became a leading voice in the movement for nuclear disarmament. Einstein supported the establishment of a world government as a means to ensure global peace and prevent future conflicts. He believed that a supranational authority was necessary to prevent the kind of catastrophic wars that had ravaged the world twice in his lifetime.

Einstein was also involved in various humanitarian efforts, supporting refugees and displaced persons affected by the war. He used his influence to raise funds and awareness for these causes, demonstrating his deep commitment to alleviating human suffering.

Einstein's work at the Institute for Advanced Study in Princeton allowed him to continue exploring the frontiers of theoretical physics, while his advocacy for civil rights and world peace demonstrated his deep commitment to humanity. These years solidified Einstein's legacy not only as a scientific genius but also as a moral and ethical leader in the global community. His time in the United States was characterized by a relentless pursuit of knowledge, a deep sense of social responsibility, and a profound commitment to using his influence for the greater good.

> **Fun Fact**
>
> In 1946, Einstein gave a famous speech at Lincoln University, a historically black university in Pennsylvania, where he received an honorary degree and spoke out against racial prejudice.

7

Later Years and Legacy (1945-1955)

Post-war Activities and Continued Scientific Pursuits

After the end of World War II, Albert Einstein remained an influential figure in both the scientific community and public life. At the Institute for Advanced Study in Princeton, he continued his quest for a unified field theory, striving to find a single framework that could encompass both general relativity and electromagnetism.

This quest for a unified theory was driven by Einstein's belief in a deterministic universe governed by consistent laws. Despite the significant challenge this posed, he dedicated much of his later years to this endeavor.

Einstein continued to publish scientific papers and correspond with colleagues around the world. He remained a prominent figure at scientific conferences

Niels Bohr

and symposia, where his ideas were both respected and debated. His persistent efforts to develop a unified field theory were a testament to his enduring passion for uncovering the fundamental principles of nature. Although he did not succeed in his lifetime, his work provided valuable insights and stimulated further research in theoretical physics.

> **Fun Fact**
> Even in his later years, Einstein would often work on complex equations and theories while playing the violin, finding that the music helped him think more clearly.

In addition to his work on the unified field theory, Einstein remained engaged with the broader developments in physics. He was particularly interested in the advancements in quantum mechanics, though he maintained his philosophical objections to its probabilistic nature. His famous debates with Niels Bohr continued through correspondence and publications, highlighting the ongoing tension between deterministic and probabilistic interpretations of physical phenomena.

Public Figure and Advocate for Peace and International Cooperation

Einstein's influence extended far beyond the realm of science. He became an ardent advocate for peace and international cooperation, using his fame and authority to promote these causes. Deeply affected by the devastation of World War II and the potential for even greater destruction in the nuclear age, Einstein spoke out against militarism and the arms race. He was a co-founder of the Emergency Committee of Atomic Scientists, an organization dedicated to informing the public about the dangers of nuclear weapons and advocating for their control and eventual elimination.

Einstein supported the establishment of the United Nations and believed in the necessity of a supranational governing body to maintain world peace. He corresponded with political leaders, participated in public debates, and wrote extensively on issues related to peace, disarmament, and human rights. His advocacy was driven by a profound sense of moral responsibility and his belief in the potential for humanity to achieve a more just and peaceful world.

In addition to his work for peace, Einstein was a vocal supporter of civil rights. He continued his active support for African American civil rights organizations and maintained his friendships with prominent civil rights leaders such as W.E.B. Du Bois and Paul Robeson. His home in Princeton was a haven for intellectuals and activists, reflecting his inclusive and egalitarian values.

Einstein's advocacy for civil rights extended to his support for the anti-lynching movement and his public denouncements of racial segregation in the United States. He saw the fight against racial injustice as integral to his broader commitment to human rights and dignity. His outspoken stance on these issues was both courageous and influential, particularly at a time when such views were not widely accepted.

> **Fun Fact**
> Einstein's fame and moral authority were such that in 1952, he was offered the presidency of Israel. He declined, citing his lack of experience in political matters and his desire to focus on scientific work and advocacy for peace.

Role in the Development of Atomic Energy and the Manhattan Project

Einstein's years in America coincided with a period of rapid advancements in nuclear physics. Although Einstein himself was not directly involved in the technical development of nuclear weapons, his famous equation, E=mc2E=mc^2E=mc2, laid the theoretical foundation for the conversion of mass into energy, a principle crucial to the development of atomic bombs.

Einstein and Oppenheimer

In 1939, concerned about the potential for Nazi Germany to develop nuclear weapons, Einstein signed a letter to President Franklin D. Roosevelt, drafted by physicist Leo Szilard. This letter urged the United States to accelerate its own atomic research, leading to the establishment of the Manhattan Project. The Manhattan Project was a top-secret U.S. government research initiative aimed at developing the first nuclear weapons. Although Einstein did not work on the project himself, his letter is often credited with spurring the U.S. government to prioritize nuclear research.

Einstein later expressed regret about his indirect role in the development of nuclear weapons, advocating for the

> **Fun Fact**
> Despite his pivotal role in alerting the U.S. government to the potential of nuclear weapons, Einstein was not granted the necessary security clearance to work on the Manhattan Project, largely due to his pacifist views and left-leaning political beliefs.

responsible use of atomic energy and emphasizing the need for international cooperation to prevent nuclear proliferation. He became an active voice in the movement for nuclear disarmament, recognizing the devastating potential of the weapons he had inadvertently helped bring into existence.

Manhattan Project Emblem

Health Issues and Final Years

As Einstein aged, he began to experience health problems. In 1948, he underwent surgery to repair an abdominal aortic aneurysm, a serious condition that would ultimately contribute to his death. Despite his health issues, Einstein remained active in his scientific and humanitarian pursuits. He continued to correspond with colleagues, work on theoretical problems, and speak out on political and social issues.

Einstein's health continued to decline steadily in his final years. Nevertheless, he remained intellectually active and committed to his work. On April 17, 1955, Einstein experienced internal bleeding caused by the rupture of his aneurysm. He was admitted to Princeton Hospital but refused surgery, believing that he had lived a full life and that it was his time to go. He passed away early the next morning on April 18, 1955, at the age of 76.

Even in his final moments, Einstein's mind was on science. He was reported to have been working on a speech he was to deliver on Israeli independence. His commitment to both his

> **Fun Fact**
> Einstein's brain was removed during the autopsy without his family's permission, a controversial action that led to decades of study. Researchers hoped to uncover the secrets of his extraordinary intellect.

scientific pursuits and his humanitarian ideals was unwavering until the very end.

Death and the Enduring Legacy of His Work and Ideas

Einstein's death marked the end of an era, but his legacy continued to grow. His contributions to science, particularly his theories of relativity, revolutionized our understanding of the universe and paved the way for numerous advancements in physics. His work on the photoelectric effect laid the groundwork for quantum mechanics, a field that has profoundly impacted technology and our understanding of the microcosm.

Beyond his scientific achievements, Einstein's advocacy for peace, civil rights, and international cooperation left a lasting impact on the world. His moral and ethical stances continue to inspire people across the globe. He is remembered not only as a brilliant scientist but also as a humanitarian who used his influence to promote justice and understanding.

Einstein's life and work have been celebrated in countless books, films, and articles. His name has become synonymous with genius, and his image—characterized by his distinctive wild hair and thoughtful expression—remains iconic. The principles he espoused and the discoveries he made continue to

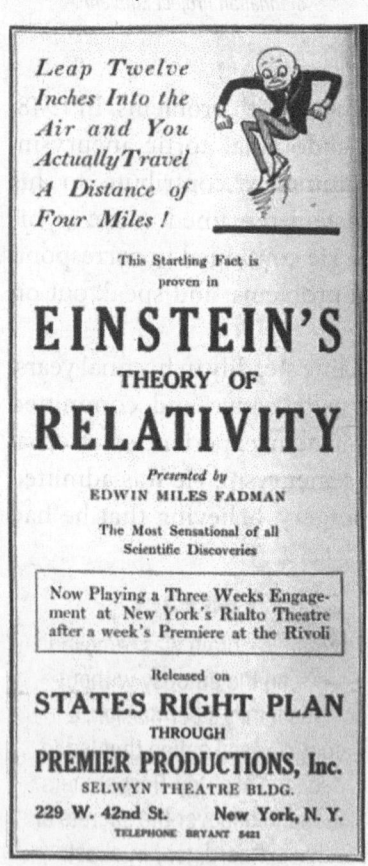

The Einstein Theory of Relativity (1923)

influence and inspire scientists, policymakers, and thinkers.

The legacy of Albert Einstein is multifaceted. Scientifically, his theories of relativity fundamentally changed our understanding of space, time, and gravity, influencing everything from the development of GPS technology to the study of black holes and the expansion of the universe. His work on the photoelectric effect was instrumental in the development of quantum mechanics, which has led to numerous technological advancements, including semiconductors and quantum computing.

Einstein's contributions to science are matched by his humanitarian legacy. His outspoken advocacy for peace, his efforts to curb nuclear proliferation, and his support for civil rights have left an indelible mark on history. His ethical stance on these issues, grounded in a deep sense of justice and compassion, continues to resonate today.

Einstein's personal papers and scientific manuscripts are preserved at the Hebrew University of Jerusalem, which he helped establish. These documents provide invaluable insights into his thought processes and the development of his groundbreaking theories. The Albert Einstein Archives serve as a testament to his enduring legacy and his lasting influence on both science and society.

> **Fun Fact**
>
> Einstein's handwritten letters and manuscripts often fetch high prices at auctions, reflecting both his historical significance and the enduring fascination with his work and personality.

From 1945 to 1955, Albert Einstein's later years were marked by continued scientific exploration, profound advocacy for peace and justice, and the inevitable challenges of aging and health issues. His death in 1955 did not diminish the impact of his work and ideas; instead, it marked the beginning of his enduring legacy as one of history's greatest minds and a champion of humanitarian causes. His time in the United States was characterized by a relentless pursuit of knowledge, a deep sense of social responsibility, and a profound commitment to using his influence for the greater good.

8
Personal Life and Character

Relationships with Family and Friends

Albert Einstein's personal life was as complex and multifaceted as his scientific theories. His relationships with family and friends were marked by both affection and conflict, reflecting the many dimensions of his character.

Einstein married his first wife, Mileva Marić, in 1903. Mileva was a fellow physicist whom Einstein met while studying at the Zurich Polytechnic. They had two sons, Hans Albert and Eduard, and possibly a daughter, Lieserl, whose fate remains uncertain. Although Einstein and Mileva shared a passion for science, their marriage was troubled. Einstein's intense focus on his work and his frequent absences strained their relationship, leading to their separation in 1914 and eventual divorce in 1919. Einstein's letters reveal a man who struggled to balance his familial responsibilities with his scientific pursuits.

Einstein maintained close friendships with several

Marcel Grossmann

prominent scientists and intellectuals throughout his life. His friendship with mathematician Marcel Grossmann, whom he met during his student days, was particularly significant. Grossmann's expertise in mathematics helped Einstein develop the mathematical foundation for the general theory of relativity. Another important friendship was with physicist Max Planck, who supported Einstein's work and helped him secure academic positions.

Portrait of Albert Einstein, Niels Bohr, James Franck and Rabi

Einstein's correspondence with other scientists, such as Niels Bohr, Werner Heisenberg, and Erwin Schrödinger, reflects his deep engagement with the scientific community. These relationships were often marked by intense intellectual exchanges and mutual respect, despite occasional disagreements.

Outside the scientific community, Einstein had friendships with numerous cultural and political figures. His relationship with Indian philosopher and Nobel laureate Rabindranath Tagore

Rabindranath Tagore with Albert Einstein

was marked by profound discussions on science, spirituality, and philosophy. He also developed a close friendship with American civil rights leader W.E.B. Du Bois, reflecting his commitment to social justice.

Einstein's personal life was not without its challenges, however. His relationship with his sons, Hans Albert and Eduard, was sometimes strained, particularly during his divorce from Mileva and the subsequent remarriage to Elsa. Despite his best intentions, Einstein's preoccupation with his work often left little time for his family, and he struggled to balance his professional and personal obligations.

Personality Traits and Habits

Einstein's personality was a fascinating blend of traits that made him both a revered genius and a beloved, albeit sometimes exasperating, figure to those around him. He was known for his intense curiosity, profound intellectual insight, and deep concentration, which often led him to become so absorbed in his thoughts that he seemed oblivious to the world around him.

> **Fun Fact**
> Despite his serious demeanor, Einstein enjoyed playing the role of the "absent-minded professor" and often used humor to connect with friends and family.

Einstein was renowned for his sense of humor and his ability to laugh at himself. He often used humor to diffuse tense situations and to put others at ease. His playful nature was evident in his interactions with children and in his love of simple, joyful activities.

Despite his joviality, Einstein could also be remarkably stubborn and independent-minded. He was known for challenging authority and conventional wisdom, both in science and in broader societal matters. His willingness to question established norms was a driving force behind his groundbreaking scientific discoveries.

Einstein's daily habits reflected his minimalist approach to life. He famously disliked wearing socks and often went without them, even in formal settings. He preferred simple, comfortable clothing and often wore the same outfits repeatedly, valuing practicality over fashion. This simplicity extended to his diet; he enjoyed modest meals and was known to be a relatively indifferent eater.

Einstein's work habits were rigorous and disciplined. He maintained a strict schedule, dedicating specific hours of the day to his scientific work. He often worked late into the night, finding the quiet hours conducive to deep thinking.

> **Fun Fact**
> Einstein's love for ice cream and his sweet tooth were well-known to his friends and family. He would often indulge in ice cream as a treat.

Despite his intense focus on work, he also valued relaxation and took breaks to play music or go for walks.

Einstein on a Picnic

Einstein's intensity and single-mindedness in pursuing his scientific interests sometimes led to social awkwardness. He could be oblivious to social niceties and occasionally came across as aloof or distant. However, those who knew him well appreciated his warmth, kindness, and genuine concern for others.

Hobbies and Interests Outside of Science

Beyond his scientific pursuits, Einstein had a rich array of hobbies and interests that provided him with joy and relaxation. One of his greatest passions was music. He was an accomplished violinist and often found solace in playing the instrument. Music was a constant companion throughout his life, and he frequently played chamber music with friends and colleagues. For Einstein, music was not only a source of personal enjoyment but also a way to connect with others and to find inspiration.

Einstein's love for music was deeply rooted in his childhood. His mother, Pauline, was a talented pianist, and she introduced him to the violin at a young age. Throughout his life, Einstein played the violin regularly, often turning to it when he needed a break from his scientific work. He particularly enjoyed the works of Mozart and Bach, whom he regarded as the epitome of musical genius.

Visiting Technion; where he planted the first palm tree

In addition to music, Einstein had a profound appreciation for nature. He loved spending time outdoors and found great pleasure in sailing. Sailing trips provided him with a peaceful escape from his demanding work and allowed him to engage with the natural world. Despite being a somewhat inept sailor—he admitted to not being very skilled at navigating—Einstein cherished the freedom and tranquility he found on the water.

Einstein was also an avid reader with a wide range of literary interests. He enjoyed reading classical literature, philosophy, and books on social and political issues. His favorite authors included Johann Wolfgang von Goethe, Leo Tolstoy, and Fyodor Dostoevsky. These works influenced his thinking and provided him with a broader perspective on human nature and society.

Einstein's interest in philosophy was more than a casual hobby. He engaged deeply with philosophical questions, particularly those related to the nature of reality, ethics, and the relationship between science and philosophy. He corresponded with several prominent philosophers, including Bertrand Russell, and often participated in philosophical discussions.

Einstein's passion for humanitarian causes was another significant aspect of his personal life. He was deeply committed to social justice and used his fame to advocate for various causes. He was a member of several civil rights organizations and supported efforts to combat racism and promote equality. His involvement in these causes reflected his belief in the importance of human dignity and his commitment to using his influence for the greater good.

Albert Einstein's personal life and character were as extraordinary as his scientific achievements. His relationships with family and friends, his unique personality traits and habits, and his diverse interests outside of science all

> **Fun Fact**
> Einstein had a peculiar fondness for playing the violin while thinking about complex scientific problems. He believed that the music helped him to relax and to think more creatively.

contributed to the rich tapestry of his life. He was a man of deep intellect and profound curiosity, yet he also possessed a playful and compassionate nature that endeared him to many. His legacy extends beyond his groundbreaking contributions to physics; it includes his humanity, his advocacy for justice, and his enduring impact on the world.

Einstein's ability to blend rigorous scientific inquiry with a deep sense of moral responsibility serves as an inspiration to people across the globe. His life story reminds us that great minds can also possess great hearts, and that the pursuit of knowledge can be harmoniously combined with the pursuit of a better world.

9

Impact on Science and Society

Einstein's Contributions to Physics and Their Lasting Significance

Albert Einstein's contributions to physics are monumental and have had a profound and lasting impact on the scientific community. His groundbreaking theories revolutionized our understanding of the universe and fundamentally altered the course of physics.

1. Special Theory of Relativity: Published in 1905, Einstein's Special Theory of Relativity introduced revolutionary concepts, including the

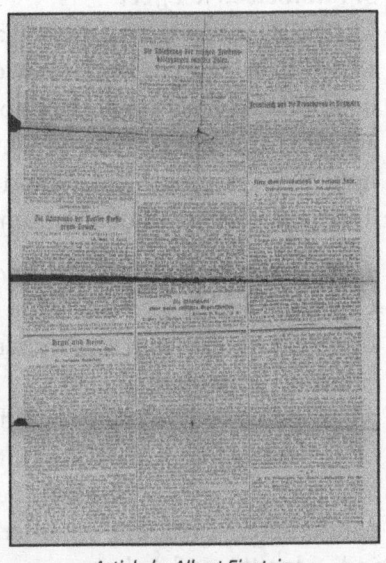

Article by Albert Einstein: My response to the Anti Relativity Theory

equivalence of mass and energy (expressed by the famous equation $E=mc2E=mc^2E=mc2$) and the relativity of simultaneity. This theory laid the foundation for modern physics, challenging long-held Newtonian concepts of space and time. It provided a new framework for understanding the behavior of objects moving at speeds close to the speed of light.

2. General Theory of Relativity:

Building upon the Special Theory of Relativity, Einstein developed the General Theory of Relativity, which he published in 1915. This theory proposed a radically new understanding of gravity, describing it as the curvature of spacetime caused by the presence of mass and energy. The General Theory of Relativity predicted phenomena such as gravitational time dilation, gravitational lensing, and the existence of black holes. It has since been confirmed through numerous experiments and observations, becoming one of the most successful theories in the history of science.

3. Photoelectric Effect:

In 1905, Einstein also published a paper on the photoelectric effect, which provided compelling evidence for the quantum nature of light. His explanation of the photoelectric effect, for which he was awarded the Nobel Prize in Physics in 1921, demonstrated that light behaves as both a wave and a particle, laying the groundwork for the development of quantum mechanics.

4 Bose-Einstein Statistics and the Theory of Bose-Einstein Condensates:

In collaboration with the Indian physicist Satyendra Nath Bose, Einstein developed the theory of Bose-Einstein statistics. This work, published in 1924, provided a fundamental understanding of the behavior of particles with integer spin, such as photons and certain types of atoms. The prediction of the Bose-Einstein condensate, a state of matter in which particles lose their individuality and behave as a single quantum entity, was later experimentally confirmed, leading to significant advances in the field of atomic physics.

5. Unified Field Theory:

Throughout his later years, Einstein pursued the elusive goal of a unified field theory, which aimed to describe all fundamental forces of nature within a single framework. Although he never fully realized this ambition, his efforts inspired subsequent generations of physicists and laid the groundwork for the development of modern theories such as string theory and quantum gravity.

Einstein's theories not only revolutionized our understanding of the physical world but also laid the groundwork for many technological advancements, including the development of nuclear energy, GPS systems, and advanced cosmological theories.

Influence on Subsequent Scientific Research and Popular Culture

Einstein's work continues to influence scientific research across a wide range of disciplines, from cosmology and particle physics to quantum mechanics and gravitational wave astronomy. His theories provide the conceptual framework for much of modern physics and have inspired generations of scientists to explore the deepest mysteries of the universe.

1. *Cosmology:*
Einstein's General Theory of Relativity revolutionized our understanding of the cosmos. It provided the theoretical

At the Yerkes Observatory

foundation for the Big Bang theory, which describes the origin and evolution of the universe. His equations have been instrumental in the study of black holes, gravitational waves, and the structure of spacetime.

2. Quantum Mechanics:

While Einstein was initially skeptical of certain aspects of quantum mechanics, his work on the photoelectric effect and the development of the theory of Bose-Einstein statistics contributed significantly to the early development of quantum theory. Today, his insights continue to inspire research into the fundamental nature of reality and the behavior of subatomic particles.

3. Gravitational Wave Astronomy:

Einstein's prediction of the existence of gravitational waves, made in 1916 as a consequence of his General Theory of Relativity, was one of the most remarkable predictions in the history of physics. In 2015, over a century after Einstein's prediction, the Laser Interferometer Gravitational-Wave Observatory (LIGO) detected gravitational waves for the first time, confirming Einstein's theory and opening a new era of gravitational wave astronomy.

4. Particle Physics:

Einstein's work on the relationship between mass and energy paved the way for the development of particle physics. His famous equation $E=mc2E=mc^2E=mc2$ is a fundamental principle in particle physics, providing the theoretical underpinning for nuclear reactions and the behavior of subatomic particles.

5. Popular Culture:

Einstein's iconic image and his status as the epitome of genius have made him a cultural icon. His name has become synonymous with intelligence and innovation. His theories and distinctive appearance have been referenced and caricatured in countless books, films, and television shows, contributing to his enduring popularity in popular culture.

Einstein's profound impact on both science and society transcends the boundaries of academia, inspiring people from all walks of life to explore the wonders of the universe and to embrace the spirit of curiosity and inquiry.

Reflections on His Philosophical and Ethical Views

In addition to his groundbreaking scientific contributions, Einstein was also known for his philosophical and ethical views, which continue to be the subject of much discussion and debate.

1. Philosophy of Science:
Einstein's approach to science was deeply philosophical. He believed in the importance of intuition and imagination in the scientific process, famously stating, "Imagination is more important than knowledge." He emphasized the role of simplicity and elegance in scientific theories, advocating for a unified and coherent understanding of the natural world.

2. Religion and Philosophy:
Einstein's views on religion and philosophy were complex and nuanced. While he rejected traditional religious dogma, he expressed a deep reverence for the beauty and harmony of the natural world, often using the language of spirituality to describe the mysteries of the universe. He famously remarked, "Science without religion is lame, religion without science is blind."

3. Ethics and Social Justice:
Einstein was a vocal advocate for social justice and human rights. He was an outspoken critic of war, militarism, and nationalism, and he actively campaigned for peace and disarmament. Throughout his life, he used his platform to

> **Fun Fact**
> Einstein's brain was preserved after his death for scientific study. Researchers have conducted various studies on his brain to understand the anatomical basis of his extraordinary cognitive abilities.

champion causes such as civil rights, freedom of expression, and international cooperation.

4. Global Citizenship:
Einstein's vision of global citizenship emphasized the interconnectedness of humanity and the importance of collective responsibility. He believed that individuals have a moral obligation to work towards the betterment of society and to strive for a more just and equitable world.

Einstein's philosophical and ethical views continue to inspire people around the world to engage with the deeper questions of existence and to strive for a more enlightened and compassionate society.

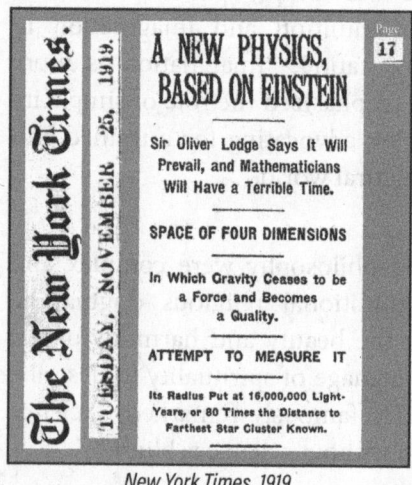

New York Times, 1919

Albert Einstein's impact on science and society is immeasurable. His revolutionary theories reshaped our understanding of the universe and paved the way for some of the most significant scientific discoveries of the modern era. Beyond his scientific achievements, Einstein's philosophical insights and ethical principles continue to inspire generations of thinkers, activists, and visionaries. His legacy serves as a testament to the power of human intellect and imagination, reminding us of the boundless potential of the human spirit to unlock the mysteries of the cosmos and to strive for a better, more enlightened world.

10

Einstein's Impact on Education and Outreach

Albert Einstein was deeply committed to the dissemination of knowledge and the promotion of scientific understanding among people of all backgrounds. Throughout his life, he actively engaged in educational initiatives aimed at fostering curiosity and critical thinking. Einstein believed that education was essential for the advancement of society and the cultivation of informed citizens.

Einstein's commitment to education stemmed from his belief that everyone, regardless of their background, should have access to knowledge and learning opportunities. He recognized the importance of making science accessible and engaging to a wide audience, not just to academics and specialists. His efforts in education and outreach were driven by a desire to inspire future generations and to instill a sense of wonder and curiosity about the natural world.

Creation of Educational Initiatives and Programs

1. Einstein's Educational Philosophy: Einstein advocated for an interdisciplinary approach to education that emphasized the interconnectedness of different fields of knowledge. He believed in the importance of fostering creativity, imagination, and independent thinking in students. Einstein's educational philosophy emphasized hands-on learning, critical inquiry, and the pursuit of intellectual curiosity.

2. *The Einstein Lectures:* Throughout his career, Einstein delivered numerous public lectures aimed at audiences ranging from school children to academics. These lectures covered a wide range of topics, including the principles of relativity, the nature of light, and the fundamental laws of physics. Einstein's lectures were renowned for their clarity, wit, and ability to captivate audiences of all ages.

3. *Educational Outreach Programs:*
Einstein was involved in the establishment of various educational outreach programs designed to bring science education to underserved communities. He supported initiatives that provided resources, materials, and educational opportunities to schools, libraries, and community centers. These programs aimed to inspire a new generation of scientists and to promote scientific literacy among the general public.

4. *The Einstein Youth Forum:*
In 1925, Einstein founded the Einstein Youth Forum, an organization dedicated to promoting science education and fostering intellectual curiosity among young people. The forum provided a platform for students to engage in scientific discussions, attend lectures, and participate in hands-on experiments. It aimed to cultivate a love for learning and a spirit of inquiry among youth from diverse backgrounds.

Einstein's Public Lectures and Engagement with the Broader Community

1. Public Lectures and Speaking Engagements:
Einstein was a prolific public speaker and lecturer, known for his engaging and accessible presentations on complex scientific topics. He traveled extensively, delivering lectures at universities, schools, and public forums around the world. Einstein's lectures attracted large and diverse audiences, ranging from fellow scientists to curious members of the public.

2. Engagement with Schools and Educational Institutions:
Einstein frequently visited schools and educational institutions to interact with students and teachers. He believed in the importance of inspiring young minds and often took the time to answer questions, conduct demonstrations, and share his enthusiasm for science. Einstein's visits to schools sparked excitement and curiosity among students, leaving a lasting impression on many aspiring scientists.

3. Public Discussions and Debates:
Einstein actively participated in public discussions and debates on scientific, social, and ethical issues. He believed in the importance of engaging with the broader community and sharing his perspectives on a wide range of topics. Einstein's willingness to engage in public discourse helped to demystify science and make it more accessible to the general public.

The Establishment of the Albert Einstein Foundation and Other Educational Endeavors

1. The Albert Einstein Foundation:
In 1936, Einstein established the Albert Einstein Foundation, a nonprofit organization dedicated to advancing education, science, and humanitarian causes. The foundation supported research, scholarship programs, and educational initiatives aimed at promoting excellence in science and fostering international cooperation.

2. Einstein's Educational Essays and Publications:
Einstein wrote extensively on the importance of education and the role of scientists in society. His essays and articles, published in newspapers, magazines, and academic journals, addressed a wide range of topics, including the philosophy of education, the social responsibility of scientists, and the need for global cooperation in advancing knowledge and understanding.

3. Legacy of Educational Initiatives:

The legacy of Einstein's educational initiatives continues to inspire educators, scientists, and policymakers around the world. His commitment to education and outreach has had a lasting impact on science education and public engagement with scientific issues. Today, the Albert Einstein Foundation continues to support educational programs and initiatives that uphold Einstein's vision of a more enlightened and intellectually curious society.

Albert Einstein's impact on education and outreach was as significant as his contributions to theoretical physics. His dedication to making science accessible, engaging, and relevant to people of all ages and backgrounds helped to inspire generations of students, educators, and science enthusiasts. Einstein's belief in the power of education to transform lives and society continues to resonate today, reminding us of the importance of fostering curiosity, critical thinking, and a lifelong love of learning.

> **Fun Fact**
> Einstein's public lectures often drew large crowds, with people lining up hours in advance to secure a seat. His engaging speaking style and ability to simplify complex concepts made him a sought-after speaker at universities and public events around the world.

11
Einstein's Views on Politics and Social Issues

Einstein's Political Activism and Advocacy for Social Justice

Albert Einstein was not only a brilliant scientist but also a passionate advocate for political and social causes. Throughout his life, he used his platform and intellectual influence to speak out against injustice, oppression, and violence. Einstein firmly believed that scientists had a moral responsibility to engage with the pressing issues of their time and to use their knowledge and influence for the betterment of society.

Involvement in Pacifist and Anti-War Movements

1. Pacifism and Anti-War Activism:
Einstein was a dedicated pacifist who actively campaigned for peace and disarmament. He was deeply troubled by the devastating impact of war and violence on humanity and was determined to do everything in his power to prevent future conflicts. Einstein believed that war was not only morally reprehensible but also fundamentally irrational, as it represented a failure of diplomacy and reason.

2. League of Nations and Internationalism:
Einstein was a vocal supporter of the League of Nations, the

predecessor to the United Nations, which he saw as a crucial mechanism for promoting international cooperation and preventing armed conflict. He advocated for the establishment of a world government based on the principles of democracy, justice, and equality. Einstein believed that only through collective action and international cooperation could lasting peace be achieved.

Views on Socialism, Democracy, and Human Rights

1. Socialism and Economic Justice:
Einstein was a staunch advocate of socialism and believed in the need for a more equitable distribution of wealth and resources. He saw capitalism as inherently exploitative and argued that socialism offered a more just and humane alternative. Einstein believed that the state should play a central role in ensuring the well-being of all citizens and in addressing the social and economic inequalities inherent in capitalist societies.

2. Democracy and Civil Liberties:
Einstein was a strong supporter of democratic principles and civil liberties. He believed in the importance of individual freedom, political participation, and the rule of law. Einstein was deeply concerned about the rise of totalitarian regimes and the erosion of democratic values in Europe during the early 20th century. He spoke out against censorship, political repression, and the curtailment of civil rights, warning of the dangers posed by authoritarianism and tyranny.

3. Human Rights and Social Justice:
Einstein was a passionate advocate for human rights and social justice. He condemned racism, discrimination, and oppression in all its forms and was an outspoken critic of colonialism and imperialism. Einstein believed that all human beings were entitled to dignity, equality, and respect, regardless of race, ethnicity, or nationality. He used his platform to champion causes such as civil rights, gender equality, and the rights of refugees and displaced persons.

Einstein's Criticisms of Totalitarianism and Authoritarianism

1. Opposition to Fascism and Nazism:
Einstein was an early and vocal critic of fascism and Nazism in Germany. He condemned the rise of Adolf Hitler and the Nazi party, warning of the dangers posed by their racist and authoritarian ideology. Einstein, who was of Jewish descent, was particularly concerned about the persecution of Jews and other minority groups under the Nazi regime. He spoke out against anti-Semitism and xenophobia, urging the international community to take a stand against tyranny and injustice.

2. Critique of Totalitarian Regimes:
Einstein's experiences living in Europe during a time of political upheaval and social unrest deeply influenced his views on totalitarianism and authoritarianism. He saw firsthand the devastating consequences of unchecked power and the erosion of democratic norms. Einstein believed that totalitarian regimes posed a grave threat to freedom, democracy, and human dignity and called on people everywhere to resist tyranny and oppression.

3. The Einstein Manifesto:
In 1939, Einstein and physicist Leó Szilárd co-authored the Einstein-Szilárd letter to President Franklin D. Roosevelt, urging the United States to develop atomic weapons before Nazi Germany. However, after witnessing the destructive power of nuclear weapons and the horrors of World War II, Einstein became a vocal advocate for nuclear disarmament and the peaceful resolution of conflicts. In 1946, he signed the Russell-Einstein Manifesto, which called for an end to the arms race and the prevention of nuclear war.

Albert Einstein's views on politics and social issues were informed by his deep sense of moral responsibility and his unwavering commitment to justice and human dignity. He believed that science and reason could be powerful tools for promoting peace, equality, and social progress. Einstein's advocacy for pacifism, democracy, socialism, and human rights continues to

> **Fun Fact**
>
> Einstein's political activism and advocacy for social justice often drew criticism and condemnation from political opponents and government authorities. Despite facing backlash and persecution, Einstein remained steadfast in his convictions and continued to speak out against injustice and oppression until the end of his life.

inspire people around the world to work towards a more just, peaceful, and compassionate society.

12

Einstein's Influence on Modern Cosmology and Astrophysics

Albert Einstein's contributions to our understanding of the cosmos have profoundly shaped modern cosmology and astrophysics. His groundbreaking work, particularly his theory of general relativity, revolutionized our understanding of the universe and laid the foundation for many of the key concepts in contemporary astrophysical research.

Albert Einstein, Pieter Zeeman, and Paul Ehrenfest

Einstein's Contributions to Our Understanding of the Cosmos

Albert Einstein's most significant contribution to cosmology was his theory of general relativity, published in 1915. This theory fundamentally transformed our understanding of gravity and the nature of spacetime, providing a new framework for interpreting the structure and dynamics of the universe.

1. General Theory of Relativity:

Einstein's theory of general relativity introduced the concept of spacetime as a dynamic, curved manifold influenced by the presence of mass and energy. This revolutionary idea led to several key developments in modern cosmology:

- **Curved Spacetime and Gravity:** Einstein's theory described gravity not as a force acting at a distance, as in Newtonian mechanics, but as the curvature of spacetime caused by the presence of matter. This concept revolutionized our understanding of gravity, providing a geometric interpretation of the gravitational force.
- **The Expanding Universe:** General relativity predicted that the universe is not static but rather expanding. Einstein initially introduced a cosmological constant to his equations to maintain a static universe, but later abandoned it when Edwin Hubble's observations confirmed the expansion of the cosmos. This insight laid the groundwork for the Big Bang theory, which describes the origin and evolution of the universe.
- **Black Holes:** Einstein's theory also predicted the existence of black holes—regions of spacetime where gravitational forces are so strong that nothing, not even light, can escape. Black holes are now a central concept in astrophysics, with observations of their effects providing strong evidence for the existence of these enigmatic objects.

Impact of General Relativity on Modern Cosmological Theories

General relativity has had a profound impact on modern cosmological theories, shaping our understanding of the structure, dynamics, and evolution of the universe.

1. Curved Spacetime and Gravity:
Einstein's theory introduced the concept of curved spacetime, providing a geometric framework for understanding the gravitational interaction between massive objects. This has led to significant advancements in our understanding of:
- *Gravitational Lensing:* According to general relativity, massive objects can bend the path of light rays as they pass through spacetime. This effect, known as gravitational lensing, has been observed and confirmed through astronomical observations. Gravitational lensing provides a powerful tool for studying the distribution of mass in the universe and probing the nature of dark matter and dark energy.
- *Gravitational Time Dilation:* General relativity predicts that time runs more slowly in regions of strong gravitational fields. This phenomenon, known as gravitational time dilation, has been confirmed through experiments and observations. For example, time runs slightly slower on Earth's surface compared to at higher altitudes, as predicted by general relativity.

2. The Expanding Universe:
Einstein's theory of general relativity predicts that the universe is expanding, a concept that has been supported by numerous astronomical observations. This insight has led to the development of the Big Bang theory, which describes the origin and evolution of the universe from a hot, dense state to its current large-scale structure. Key developments include:
- *Cosmic Microwave Background Radiation:* The Big Bang theory predicts the existence of cosmic microwave background radiation (CMB), which is the afterglow of the hot, dense early universe. The discovery of the CMB in 1965 provided strong

evidence in support of the Big Bang model and confirmed many key predictions of general relativity.
- **Galaxy Redshifts:** Observations of the redshift of distant galaxies, first made by Edwin Hubble in the 1920s, provide further evidence for the expansion of the universe. The observed redshifts are consistent with the predictions of general relativity and the expanding universe model.

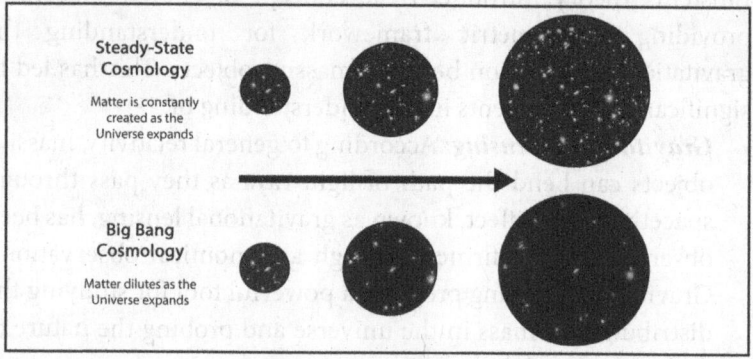

Big Bang and Steady-State Theory

3. Black Holes:

Einstein's theory of general relativity predicted the existence of black holes—regions of spacetime where gravitational forces are so strong that nothing, not even light, can escape. Black holes are now a central concept in astrophysics, with observations of their effects providing strong evidence for the existence of these enigmatic objects. Key developments include:

- **Observational Evidence:** Observations of stars orbiting around invisible objects, as well as the detection of intense X-ray and radio emissions from compact, dense objects, provide strong evidence for the presence of black holes. The behavior of matter and light around these objects is consistent with the predictions of general relativity.
- **Gravitational Waves:** In 2015, the Laser Interferometer Gravitational-Wave Observatory (LIGO) made the first direct detection of gravitational waves, confirming a key prediction of general relativity. Gravitational waves are ripples in spacetime

caused by the acceleration of massive objects, such as black holes and neutron stars. The detection of gravitational waves has opened a new window onto the universe and provided astronomers with a powerful tool for studying black holes and other astrophysical phenomena.

The Ongoing Relevance of Einstein's Work in Contemporary Astrophysics and Cosmology

Einstein's work continues to play a central role in contemporary astrophysics and cosmology, shaping our understanding of the universe and inspiring new avenues of research.

1. Cosmological Models:
General relativity forms the basis of modern cosmological models, which describe the large-scale structure and evolution of the universe. Einstein's equations allow cosmologists to model the expansion of the universe, the formation of galaxies and galaxy clusters, and the distribution of dark matter and dark energy.

2. Testing Fundamental Physics:
Einstein's theory provides a framework for testing fundamental principles of physics in extreme environments, such as near black holes and in the early universe. Observations of gravitational phenomena, such as black hole mergers and the behavior of matter in strong gravitational fields, continue to provide critical tests of general relativity and alternative theories of gravity.

3. The Search for a Unified Theory:
Einstein spent much of his later years searching for a unified theory of physics—a single framework that could encompass all fundamental forces of nature. While he was not successful in his quest, his work continues to inspire research into theories such as string theory and quantum gravity, which seek to unify general relativity with quantum mechanics.

Albert Einstein's contributions to modern cosmology and astrophysics have left an indelible mark on our understanding of the cosmos. His insights into the nature of space, time, and gravity continue to shape the way we perceive the universe and inspire new generations of scientists to explore its deepest mysteries.

4. *The Study of Gravitational Waves:*
Einstein's theory predicted the existence of gravitational waves—ripples in spacetime caused by the acceleration of massive objects. The recent detection of gravitational waves by instruments like LIGO and Virgo has provided direct evidence of the phenomena predicted by general relativity. This groundbreaking discovery has opened a new era in astrophysics, allowing scientists to study the universe in an entirely new way. Gravitational wave astronomy enables the observation of previously inaccessible events, such as the merger of black holes and neutron stars, providing invaluable insights into the most extreme and energetic phenomena in the cosmos.

5. *Dark Matter and Dark Energy:*
General relativity plays a crucial role in our understanding of the universe's composition, including the mysterious dark matter and dark energy. While dark matter's presence is inferred from its gravitational effects on visible matter, dark energy is thought to be responsible for the observed accelerated expansion of the universe. Einstein's equations are used to model the distribution of dark matter and dark energy, shedding light on their properties and influence on cosmic evolution.

6. *Advanced Techniques in Observational Cosmology:*
Modern astrophysical observations and techniques heavily rely on Einstein's theories. From gravitational lensing to cosmological redshifts, many observational tools are grounded in general relativity. High-resolution telescopes, space-based observatories, and sophisticated data analysis techniques leverage Einstein's insights to probe the universe's most profound mysteries, including the cosmic microwave background radiation, large-scale structure formation, and the early universe's conditions.

7. Quantum Gravity and Fundamental Physics:

Einstein's theory of general relativity remains a cornerstone in the quest for a unified theory of physics, which reconciles gravity with quantum mechanics. The theoretical framework laid by Einstein continues to inspire physicists in their search for a theory of quantum gravity. Ideas such as string theory, loop quantum gravity, and other quantum gravity approaches are directly influenced by Einstein's work and strive to extend general relativity into the quantum realm, providing a deeper understanding of the fundamental nature of the universe.

8. Influence on Multidisciplinary Research:

Einstein's impact extends beyond the realms of physics to interdisciplinary research areas, such as astrophysics, mathematics, computer science, and philosophy. The interdisciplinary nature of modern cosmology and astrophysics often draws on the principles of general relativity to address complex questions related to the origin, evolution, and fate of the universe. Collaborative efforts between scientists from diverse fields continue to push the boundaries of our knowledge, propelled by Einstein's revolutionary insights.

Albert Einstein's enduring influence on modern cosmology and astrophysics underscores the profound significance of his contributions to our understanding of the cosmos. His theories have not only reshaped the landscape of theoretical physics but have also inspired generations of scientists to explore the universe's deepest mysteries with curiosity, rigor, and imagination.

> **Fun Fact**
>
> Einstein's theory of general relativity predicts that the universe's expansion is accelerating, driven by an enigmatic force known as dark energy. This prediction was confirmed by observations of distant supernovae in the late 1990s, leading to the Nobel Prize in Physics in 2011 being awarded to the discovery's leaders, Saul Perlmutter, Brian P. Schmidt, and Adam G. Riess.

13

Einstein's Nobel Prize and Recognition

Albert Einstein's Nobel Prize in Physics for his work on the photoelectric effect marked a significant milestone in his illustrious career and public recognition. Beyond the Nobel Prize, Einstein received numerous other awards, honors, and recognitions throughout his life, highlighting the profound impact of his scientific contributions on the world stage.

Albert Einstein's Nobel

Einstein's Nobel Prize in Physics for his Work on the Photoelectric Effect

In 1921, Albert Einstein was awarded the Nobel Prize in Physics "for his services to Theoretical Physics, and especially for his discovery of the law of the photoelectric effect." This recognition honored his pioneering work on the photoelectric effect, which laid the foundation for the quantum theory of light and significantly advanced our understanding of the nature of light and matter.

1. Discovery of the Photoelectric Effect:

- Einstein's groundbreaking paper on the photoelectric effect, published in 1905 during his "miracle year," proposed that light could be understood as consisting of discrete packets of energy called photons. This theory explained how light could eject electrons from a material's surface, a phenomenon known as the photoelectric effect.
- His explanation of the photoelectric effect revolutionized the field of quantum mechanics, challenging classical wave theory and providing compelling evidence for the quantization of light.

2. Impact of the Nobel Prize on Einstein's Career and Public Profile:

- The Nobel Prize brought Einstein international acclaim and solidified his reputation as one of the world's leading physicists. It elevated his status as a scientific luminary and propelled him into the public spotlight.
- While the Nobel Prize recognized his work on the photoelectric effect, it also served to highlight the broader significance of his scientific contributions, cementing his position as a preeminent figure in 20th-century physics.

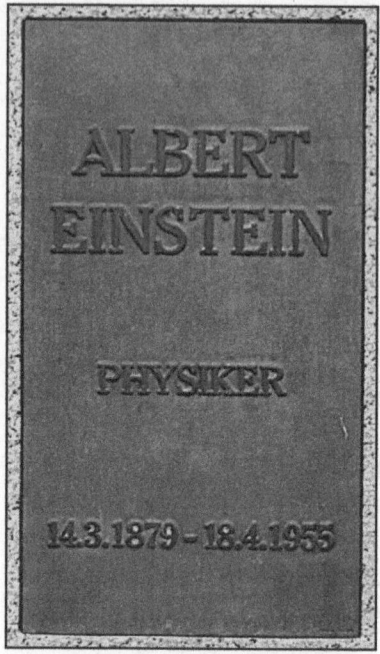
Plaque at the Bust Albert Einstein by Heinrich Drake

3. Einstein's Other Awards, Honors, and Recognition Throughout His Life:

- Copley Medal (1925): Awarded by the Royal Society of London for his contributions to theoretical physics.
- Max Planck Medal (1929): Recognized for his extraordinary achievements in theoretical physics.
- ForMemRS (1921): Elected as a Foreign Member of the Royal Society in recognition of his exceptional scientific contributions.
- Time Magazine's Person of the Century (1999): Voted as the "Person of the Century" for his revolutionary impact on science and human understanding.
- Numerous Honorary Degrees: Einstein received honorary degrees from prestigious universities around the world, including Harvard University, the University of Oxford, and the Sorbonne.

4. The Significance of Einstein's Nobel Prize in the Context of His Broader Scientific Contributions:

- While Einstein's Nobel Prize specifically recognized his work on the photoelectric effect, its significance extends far beyond this particular achievement. His broader scientific contributions, including the theory of relativity, quantum mechanics, and the equivalence of mass and energy ($E=mc^2$), reshaped the foundations of physics and our understanding of the universe.

- The Nobel Prize served as a symbol of Einstein's groundbreaking research and innovative thinking, highlighting his ability to unravel some of the most profound mysteries of the physical world.

Einstein shaking hands with a dignitary

Albert Einstein's Nobel Prize in Physics for his work on the photoelectric effect stands as a testament to his extraordinary intellect, creativity, and scientific vision. The recognition he received throughout his life, both from the Nobel Committee and other esteemed institutions, underscored the transformative impact of his scientific contributions on the course of 20th-century physics and beyond.

Einstein's Nobel Prize win in 1921 wasn't his only association with the Nobel Committee. In 1912, 1913, and 1914, he was nominated for the Nobel Prize in Physics for his work on the photoelectric effect, but he was not awarded the prize until 1921.

Fun Fact

Albert Einstein's Nobel Prize money was used to fund his divorce from his first wife, Mileva Marić, and to provide financial support to their two sons, Hans Albert and Eduard.

14

Einstein's Unfinished Work and Unanswered Questions

Albert Einstein's legacy in physics and mathematics is immense, but there are still areas where his theories remain incomplete, and numerous unsolved problems persist in theoretical physics. The ongoing efforts to extend and refine Einstein's theories reflect the profound influence he continues to have on the quest for a unified theory of fundamental forces.

Areas of Physics and Mathematics Where Einstein's Theories Remain Incomplete

1. Quantum Gravity:
- Einstein's theory of general relativity successfully describes gravity on cosmic scales but does not adequately incorporate the principles of quantum mechanics, which govern the behavior of matter and energy on the smallest scales.
- The quest for a theory of quantum gravity aims to reconcile general relativity with quantum mechanics, providing a unified framework to describe the fundamental forces of nature at both the cosmological and quantum levels.

2. Singularities in Black Holes:
- While general relativity predicts the existence of black holes—regions of spacetime with extremely strong gravitational fields—our current understanding breaks down at the singularities within black holes.
- Resolving the singularities within black holes is a major challenge in theoretical physics, requiring a quantum theory of gravity to describe the extreme conditions of these enigmatic objects.

3. *The Nature of Dark Matter and Dark Energy:*
- Einstein's equations describe the behavior of visible matter and energy but do not account for the mysterious dark matter and dark energy, which together make up the vast majority of the universe's content.
- Understanding the nature of dark matter and dark energy remains one of the most pressing unsolved problems in cosmology and requires new theoretical frameworks beyond Einstein's theories.

Unsolved Problems and Unanswered Questions in Theoretical Physics

1. *The Grand Unified Theory:*
- The Grand Unified Theory seeks to unify three of the four fundamental forces of nature—electromagnetism, the weak nuclear force, and the strong nuclear force—into a single theoretical framework.
- While significant progress has been made, a complete GUT remains elusive, with many aspects of particle physics and cosmology still unexplained.

2. *The Theory of Everything:*
- The Theory of Everything aims to unify all four fundamental forces—gravity, electromagnetism, the weak nuclear force, and the strong nuclear force—into a single, coherent framework.
- Developing a TOE is one of the most ambitious goals in theoretical physics and would represent a profound advancement in our understanding of the universe.

3. *Quantum Gravity and the Quantization of Spacetime:*
- Combining the principles of quantum mechanics with those of general relativity requires the quantization of spacetime itself.
- Developing a consistent theory of quantum gravity remains a major challenge, with many unresolved questions about the fundamental nature of space, time, and gravity.

Continuing Efforts to Extend and Refine Einstein's Theories

1. String Theory and M-Theory:
- String theory and its extension, M-theory, propose that fundamental particles are not point-like but instead are one-dimensional "strings" or higher-dimensional "branes" vibrating in a higher-dimensional spacetime.
- These theories offer promising avenues for unifying gravity with the other fundamental forces and provide a framework for addressing some of the outstanding questions in theoretical physics.

2. Loop Quantum Gravity:
- Loop quantum gravity is an approach to quantum gravity that seeks to quantize spacetime itself, treating it as a discrete network of interconnected loops.
- This approach aims to resolve the singularities in general relativity and provide a consistent quantum description of gravity.

3. Emergent Gravity and Quantum Information Theory:
- Emergent gravity posits that gravity is not a fundamental force but rather an emergent phenomenon that arises from the collective behavior of quantum information.
- By viewing gravity through the lens of quantum information theory, researchers seek to develop new insights into the nature of spacetime and the quantum structure of the universe.

Einstein's Lasting Influence on the Search for a Unified Theory of Fundamental Forces

Albert Einstein's work continues to inspire and guide the search for a unified theory of fundamental forces, despite the incomplete nature of his own theories. His profound insights into the nature of space, time, and gravity have paved the way for generations of physicists to explore the deepest mysteries of the universe.

Conclusion

Albert Einstein's life and work have left an indelible mark on the landscape of science, shaping our understanding of the universe and inspiring generations of scientists and thinkers. From his groundbreaking theories of relativity to his contributions to quantum mechanics and beyond, Einstein's intellectual curiosity, creativity, and relentless pursuit of truth have fundamentally transformed our perception of the cosmos. His revolutionary insights into the nature of space, time, and gravity, culminating in the development of the theory of general relativity, revolutionized the field of theoretical physics and laid the foundation for modern cosmology and astrophysics.

Throughout his life, Einstein remained a tireless advocate for peace, social justice, and human rights. His unwavering commitment to intellectual freedom and moral integrity served as a beacon of hope in troubled times, inspiring countless individuals to strive for a better world.

Einstein's influence extended far beyond the realm of academia, permeating popular culture and inspiring countless works of literature, art, and film. His iconic image and quotable wisdom have become synonymous with genius, symbolizing the power of human intellect and imagination to unlock the secrets of the universe.

While many of the questions Einstein grappled with remain unanswered, his legacy continues to inspire new generations of scientists to push the boundaries of human knowledge. From the search for a unified theory of fundamental forces to the exploration of the deepest mysteries of space and time, Einstein's spirit of inquiry lives on in the hearts and minds of those who dare to dream and strive for a deeper understanding of the cosmos.

As we reflect on the life and work of Albert Einstein, we are reminded of the boundless potential of the human mind and the enduring power of curiosity, creativity, and perseverance. His legacy serves as a reminder that no challenge is insurmountable and that the pursuit of truth is a noble endeavor worthy of our highest aspirations.

In the words of Einstein himself, "The most beautiful thing we can experience is the mysterious. It is the source of all true art and science. He to whom this emotion is a stranger, who can no longer pause to wonder and stand rapt in awe, is as good as dead: his eyes are closed." Albert Einstein's eyes remained open to the wonders of the universe until the end of his days, and his legacy continues to illuminate our path forward, guiding us toward a brighter, more enlightened future.

Despite his towering intellect, Einstein was known for his humility and sense of humor. He once said, "I have no special talents. I am only passionately curious." This sentiment captures the essence of his approach to life and learning—an insatiable curiosity about the world and a deep appreciation for the beauty and mystery of existence.

Albert Einstein (1879-1955) was born in Germany and became an American citizen in 1940. He was a world-famous theoretical physicist, awarded the Nobel Prize for Physics in 1921, and is renowned for his Theory of Relativity. Einstein was an influential humanist who spoke widely about politics, ethics and social causes. His theories were instrumental in shaping the atomic age.

OTHER TITLES IN THE SERIES

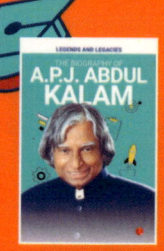

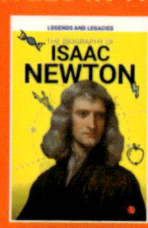

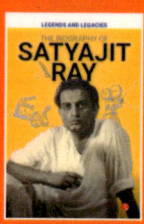

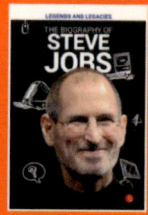

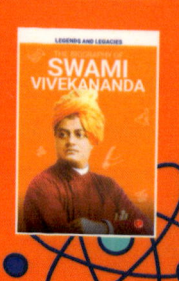

Cover design: Swar Khosla
Cover photograph: Wikimedia Commons

Also available as an e-book
Non-fiction
ISBN 978-93-6156-845-9

₹150

www.rupapublications.co.in